The Magic of Costa Rica

CONTENTS

Introduction

Tiny Costa Rica, covering a mere 51,120km² (19,739 sq miles), packs a tremendous diversity of landscape, vegetation and wildlife into its small size. Towering mountains, many of them volcanic, give way at lower levels to fertile plateaux, cloud forests, savannah cattle country and tropical swamplands. Over a quarter of the countryside is protected in some way, so it is little wonder that Costa Rica is home to over 10,000 species of plants, 240 types of mammals, 10% of the world's butterflies and 850 different species of birds. Costa Rica is recognized as a safe country and the *ticos*, as the Costa Ricans are called, are friendly and welcoming. It is not surprising, therefore, that the country has become one of the world's top eco-tourist destinations.

Above Children perform a folk dance in the province of Guanacaste. Young Costa Ricans are encouraged to learn the traditional songs and dances of their local province and frequently provide shows at tourist hotels.

Right The swallowtail is just one of a great number of butterflies found throughout Costa Rica. Over 3000 species of moths and butterflies have been found in one national park alone.

Opposite A vendor sells a coconut to a tourist at Puerto Limón's outdoor market, which has a vast array of fresh fruit and vegetables on offer.

GEOGRAPHY

The relatively recent science called plate tectonics has done much to explain the origins of Costa Rica. Some five million years ago the Cocos Plate pushed eastward against the Caribbean Plate, forming a 'collision zone' that forced up mountain ranges and squeezed out volcanic magma. This material formed a narrow isthmus of land that eventually linked the continents of North and South America. Costa Rica forms part of this ancient land bridge, which was used by wildlife, and later human beings, to colonize the area. Today, this region remains unstable and experiences frequent earthquakes and volcanic eruptions.

The mountainous spine of Costa Rica is composed of towering ranges or *cordillera*, which rise to the country's highest point of 3820m (12,533ft) at Mt Chirripó. Most of these ranges are volcanically active. Indeed, Costa Rica forms part of the Pacific Ring of Fire and currently has five

Below Reaching 3820m (12,533ft) Mt Chirripó is Costa Rica's highest mountain. Climbers have flocked here ever since a missionary priest was the first to conquer it in 1904. Although well within the tropics, glacial features can be seen on its rocky upper slopes and the vistas from the summit are spectacular.

Above Hikers tackle the boulder-strewn slopes of *Volcán Arenal*. Rising to 1633m (5358ft), Arenal is generally considered the most dangerous and unpredictable active volcano in Costa Rica, with frequent eruptions and associated earthquakes.

active volcanoes and around 60 or so extinct or dormant ones – enough to satisfy any visiting vulcanologist. Three volcanoes, in particular, have excited interest in recent years. Mt Irazú 3432m (11,260ft) erupted violently in the 1960s, destroying two seasons' coffee crops before calming down. Mt Poás 2704m (8871ft) has been active in a variety of ways since the 1950s, occasionally so dangerously that the surrounding national park had to be closed down briefly. Most spectacular of all, however, is Mt Arenal, 1633m (5358ft), which has been rumbling away for the last 35 years and can give some dramatic firework displays – best seen at night while lolling in the nearby Tabacón hot springs. While they are fascinating to tourists, volcanic eruptions have a very beneficial result for Costa Ricans – the volcanic ash, when weathered down, provides fertile soil for the country's main cash crop, coffee, plus a variety of other fruit and vegetables.

COASTLINES AND REEFS

Costa Rica's two coastlines present marked contrasts. The Caribbean coastline is short – a mere 200km (125 miles) and backed by sandy beaches, mangrove swamps and dense rainforests. Coral reefs were once common offshore, but recent earth movements have destroyed them by raising the reefs above sea level. These tectonic movements also lifted the bed of the intra coastal waterway, making navigation difficult. Tourism here remains low key.

Below Costa Rica's rainforests are magic places. Wet and humid, they reverberate with the songs of birds and the roar of howler monkeys.

The Pacific coast, in contrast, is quite a bit longer, stretching for over 1000km (620 miles). The shoreline is generally rugged, with cliffs interspersed with sandy bays, mangrove swamps and peninsulas. Because of the pronounced dry season, tourism thrives here, with some large new holiday developments, such as those at Tambor and Papagayo. Turtle nesting, whale watching and surfing add to the attractions for visitors.

Above Five species of sea turtles have their nesting grounds on Costa Rica's beaches. A few of the local people are responsible for protecting the eggs, as both these and the hatchlings face many predators. Only a small percentage of baby sea turtles reach adulthood.

CLIMATE

Costa Rica is typically subtropical in that it experiences two distinct seasons. The dry season is generally referred to as *verano* (summer) and lasts from December to April. This is the period that attracts the most tourists. The wet season or *invierno* (winter) lasts for the remainder of the year. The Costa Rican authorities have dubbed this the 'green season' and would like to extend the tourist season into this period.

The division into two seasons is in reality rather simplistic, because there are considerable variations. The Caribbean Lowlands, for example, have heavy rain throughout the year, while the highest mountains often experience frost. The Central Valley, where the capital San José is located, has what the United Nations has described as one of the most agreeable climates in the world, with a healthy 20°C (68°F) throughout the year. Many Americans now prefer to spend their winters in Costa Rica rather than in Florida.

WILDLIFE

The essence of Costa Rica's attraction is its abundant wildlife, and it has lured nature lovers from all corners of the globe. Yet it is hardly surprising that its species are so prolific, considering the variety of landscape, vegetation and climate that this small country offers, along with the amount of protection and conservation provided.

Visitors to Costa Rica should not expect to see the abundant game typical of the African plains, but nevertheless, there are some 200 species of mammals in the country. It has to be said that many of these are elusive and rare, such as the forest cats like jaguars, ocelots and pumas, but the tree-dwelling monkeys are noticeable, particularly the raucous howlers. Rather scarcer are the white-faced, spider and squirrel monkeys.

Everyone's favourites are the slow-moving sloths, of which there are two varieties in Costa Rica. Shuffling along the forest floors are many smaller mammals including the anteater, armadillo and coati.

Costa Rica boasts 162 varieties of snake, of which 22 are venomous. The good news is, though, that visitors to the country are highly unlikely to encounter any of these, generally very shy, creatures.

More obvious are the large and colourful iguanas, many of which are tame enough to reside in hotel grounds. Waterways in the rainforests are home to crocodiles and caimans but these are rarely large enough to pose a threat. Especially fascinating are the Jesus Christ lizards, which can literally 'walk on water' when disturbed.

Above Among the four species of monkeys in the country, the spider monkey with its long limbs and prehensile tail is the most acrobatic.

The beaches of Costa Rica are the nesting grounds of no fewer than five species of sea turtles. When the conditions are right they come ashore in huge numbers, an event known as an *arriba*, to lay their eggs in the sand.

In the more humid areas of Costa Rica, insects abound. The pesky mosquitos are unwelcome, but there is a host of beautiful butterflies to delight the eye. At the top of the list is the stunning blue morpho, a mobile jewel as it flits through the forest clearings. It is estimated that Costa Rica hosts around 10% of the world's butterfly species and the country supplies pupae to butterfly farms around the globe. While walking

Below The Basilisk Lizard is also known as the Jesus Christ Lizard for its ability to 'walk on water'. Web-like feet enable it to move quickly across water for about 10–20m (33–65ft) without sinking.

Above The scarlet macaw is one of Costa Rica's most colourful birds. Sadly, the number is in decline. Pairs of macaws can often be seen flying closely together with their wing tips touching.

Right The spectactular blue morpho, often seen flitting across a sunlit forest glade, is one of Costa Rica's most common butterflies. Numerous butterfly farms provide excursions for visiting eco tourists, showing all stages of the life cycle of the butterfly.

through the rainforest, keep an eye on the ground for the busy leaf cutter ants as they carry material to their nests.

An astonishing 850 species of birds have been recorded in Costa Rica, so it is hardly surprising that the country has become a Mecca for bird watchers. The birds are amazingly exotic, none more so that the resplendent quetzal, with its four-foot-long tail. Toucans, macaws, parrots, parakeets and the 50 species of hummingbirds are just a few of the other attractions. Herons, aninghas, egrets and lily trotters inhabit the forest waterways, while pelicans and frigatebirds are commonly seen offshore.

The Costa Rican government has been quick to recognize the enormous value of eco-tourism. The local national park network is very comprehensive, and eco lodges and other cheap accommodation can be found around the fringes of parks and rainforests.

FLORA

Below Costa Rica has more fern species than the whole of North America. Tree ferns go back to prehistoric times.

The World Resources Institute recently proclaimed that Costa Rica had, for its size, the most varied flora in the world. Some facts: Costa Rica has some 10,000 species of plants, with more being identified daily; over 1200 types of orchids alone have been identified; around 1400 tree species have been noted in the country and it has more species of ferns than the whole of North America.

This diversity is particularly pronounced in the rainforests of Costa Rica, where it is often possible to identify over 200 species within one acre. Of particular interest in the rainforests is the plant life that grows and depends on trees, such as epiphytes, lianas and bromeliads.

Tropical rainforests girdle the earth around the equatorial zone and are typified by continual rains and high temperatures throughout the year. The steamy atmosphere has enabled the growth of a vast range of species. The rainforests in Costa Rica, for example, have as many plant species as the whole of Europe.

Biologists have defined a series of layers in the rainforests that start with the Ground Layer and progress upwards through the Shrub Layer, the Middle Layer, the Canopy Layer and the Emergent-Tree Layer. Each of these strata has its own assemblage of plants and animals, usually in profusion.

The Ground Layer can seem very quiet and devoid of animal activity. This has encouraged naturalists to spend time in the more productive Canopy Layer and, as a result, some unusual mechanical aids have been developed in recent years. The prime example of this in Costa Rica is the Aerial Tram, the brainchild of American biologist Donald Perry. It consists of a series of open-sided overhead cable cars, which transport visitors through the canopy of the rainforest of the Braulio Carillo National Park following a 2.6km (1.6-mile) course.

Costa Rica was originally covered with vast areas of rainforest. A small proportion of these are now protected in the national park system, including the Tortuguero Park on the Caribbean coast, the small Manuel Antonio Park on the Pacific coast and the large, but remote Corcovado Park in the south-west of the country. Sadly, these areas are not free from threats, mainly from logging firms and poachers who prey on wildlife for the pet trade.

Above Costa Rica has one of the richest orchid flora in the world. The flowers vary in size from 1mm to 50cm (19.5in). Although orchids are found in all regions of the country, enthusiasts should head for the forests, where an expert claimed to have identified 47 different species growing on a single tree.

Right Costa Ricans are ethnically homogeneous with 90% of the people being of Spanish descent. The black people take up 2% and mainly live in the Limón province and less than 2% are indigenous Indians.

THE PEOPLE

Costa Rica has a vibrant population of more than 3½ million, over half of whom live in the Central Valley. Life expectancy is currently at 76.1%, while infant mortality is low. Not surprisingly, population growth has rarely been below 2% in recent decades. Ethnically, Costa Rica is homogeneous, with some 96% of the population being of Spanish descent. Around 2% are black and these are mainly confined to Limón province. They were brought over to work on the Jungle Railway and many stayed on as labourers in the banana plantations. In addition a small number of *indigenas* live on reservations, mainly in the south of the country. In recent years a number of foreigners, mainly from the USA, have settled in Costa Rica.

Right A knowledge of Spanish is helpful to the visitor, although English is widely spoken in the tourist industry.

LANGUAGE

The official language of Costa Rica is Spanish. A small number of indigenous languages survive, although only one has an alphabet. English is widely spoken in the tourist industry, which caters largely for North American holiday makers.

Right Costa Rica has many fine churches and cathedrals, although some have been damaged by earthquakes. It is a Catholic country, but all religions are tolerated.

RELIGION

The official religion of Costa Rica is Roman Catholicism, although many *ticos* merely pay it lip service. Indeed, church authorities despair of the way religious festivals have become secularized. Local saints' days are public holidays. The whole country closes down during Holy Week, when *ticos* flock to the beaches. Other religions are tolerated in Costa Rica. Most of the Caribbean blacks are Protestant and in recent years North American Mormons have gained a foothold.

FESTIVALS

The country's foremost cultural event is the annual International Arts Festival held in San José in March. It features music, dance, art exhibitions and theatre. Local festivals usually include folk song and dancing, slapstick bullfights, parades, rodeos, street theatre and the inevitable fireworks. The Carnival at Puerto Limón in October is one of the most vibrant in the Latin world. It attracts *ticos* from all over the country. The highlight is the huge street parade with outrageous costumes, ornate floats and deafening music. Although vast amounts of alcohol are usually consumed, a special alcohol-free zone is provided for families and their children.

Left The annual festival at Limón is one of the most lively *fiestas* in Central America. *Ticos* celebrate their festivals with enthusiasm, with folk songs, dancing, street parades, rodeos and beauty contests.

ARTS AND CRAFTS

Although craft shops abound in Costa Rica, particularly in the areas attractive to tourists, few of the products on sale originated in the country. Most items have been imported from neighbouring states or even further afield. The advent of tourism, however, has encouraged a renaissance of traditional crafts. This is particularly apparent in the Nicoya area where there has been a revival in the traditional pottery of the Choretega Indians. Santa Ana in the Central Valley has also seen a resurgence of ceramics, Here, some 30 family workshops have sprung up.

The craft capital of Costa Rica, however, is undoubtedly the village of Sarchí. Shops, workshops and factories line the main street, all selling the gaily painted ox carts or *carretas*. The colourful designs on the carts are thought to have originated in Andalucía and artisans can be watched in many of the workshops applying their skills. The ox carts come in various sizes, from table top to full scale. The shops in Sarchí sell a variety of other craft goods including wooden bowls, leather rocking chairs, hammocks and the ubiquitous t-shirts.

Left Straw horses at a Limón craft fair. Tourists often show an interest in local crafts and this has sparked a revival in Costa Rican handicrafts, particularly those of the *indigenas*.

Below A stall displays pottery made by the Chortega indians at Guaitil in Nicoya province. Local clay is used and traditional colours dominate.

Above Costa Rica is one of the world's top surfing spots. Beaches are not crowded and the waves are big and long. At Pavones on the south Pacific coast, the waves can be 1km (0.6214 miles) long and give a ride of up to three minutes.

SPORT

As in many countries in the world, the sporting obsession with Costa Ricans is soccer. Each village, however small, has its football pitch. The country runs two national leagues and games take place between September and June. This frees up the better footballers to play elsewhere in the world during the rest of year and many have performed creditably for British and European clubs.

Bullfighting is a comic event in Costa Rica. The bull is never killed and as many as 20 budding toreadors will enter the ring to taunt the bull, jump on its back or pull its tail. Scores of other spectators jump into the ring and equally quickly leap out if the bull heads their way! Other sports, particularly outdoor activities, are provided largely for tourists. Some of the best surfing in the world is available on the Pacific coast at Pavones, while sail boarders find ideal conditions on Lake Arenal. Snorkelling and scuba diving enthusiasts have fewer opportunities now that many of the coral reefs have been destroyed by earth movements. The best remaining reefs are in the Cahuita Marine National Park.

Below Costa Rica is an outdoor paradise. Snorkelling is possible on both the Pacific and Caribbean coasts. There are also facilities for diving, white water rafting, wind surfing, sea kayaking and sport fishing.

12

Left Red toffee apples dipped in nuts are a well-known dessert for Costa Rican children. For those who do not have a sweet tooth; there is a choice of a wide variety of fruit.

FOOD AND DRINK

Costa Rican food is simple, unpretentious and tasty, with fresh ingredients – which may be a major factor in explaining the *ticos* longevity. It relies heavily on rice and beans. For instance, a traditional breakfast dish is *gallo pinto* (spotted rooster), which consists of rice, red and black beans plus sour cream and eggs. The same ingredients reappear at lunchtime, with the addition of meat or fish, fried plantain and coleslaw, under the description *casado* (literally 'married').

Costa Rica has a generous coastline, but much of its fish harvest is exported. However, menus will generally feature sea bass, tuna and red snapper. Desserts are varied, but invariably sweet, with a plethora of recipes featuring condensed milk. Fortunately, there is a wealth of tropical fruit available, including mangoes, pineapple, pawpaws and bananas.

Below Much of the country's food is bland, being based on rice and beans. For a more spicy offering head for the Caribbean coast where Creole food is available.

Probably the most exciting food in Costa Rica is found on the Caribbean coast, where Creole cooking features coconut milk, yams, ackee, breadfruit and a range of spices. There is a wide range of drinks available, but wine lovers will be disappointed as Costa Rica has no vineyards and all wine is imported and expensive. Fortunately, there are excellent local beers, such as Imperial and Bavaria. Steer clear, however, of the local firewater, *guaro*, a spirit made from sugar cane and known for its spectacular hangovers. There are some thirst-quenching soft drinks called *frescos* that are made from fresh fruit and milk. Popular flavours are pineapple, mango and blackberry. Costa Rican coffee is superb and is exported all over the world.

International restaurants have appeared on the scene in recent years and in the larger towns such as San José it is easy to find Asian, Italian and French restaurants, plus the ubiquitous American fast-food chains. Many *ticos* prefer to eat in *sodas*, which are similar to American diners. Here, a *plato del día* will be offered at a bargain price. A dwindling number of bars provide *bocas*, a small snack similar to the Spanish *tapas*, to go with a drink. It was free a while back, now it has to be paid for.

History

PRE-COLUMBIAN TIMES

It is believed that Costa Rica was first peopled around 10,000BC, but evidence about the way of life of these groups only goes back to about 1000BC. There were apparently some 20 or 30 tribes, each led by a chief or *cacique*. They had religious beliefs and the shaman was a powerful figure. The tribes practiced subsistence farming, raising crops such as yucca and squash. They also hunted and fished. The tribes lived in fortified stockades – these were necessary as all the groups were warlike and regularly raided each other's territories to capture slaves.

Although none of the indigenous groups had a written language, they were not without skills. Some groups, such as the Chibchas, were accomplished goldsmiths, while other groups worked in jade. The Chorotegas in the Guancaste were famous for their pottery, a skill that has recently been revived. The most remarkable artefacts of this period, however, are the lithic spheres or stone balls made by the Diquis tribe. They were fashioned out of hard granite and can measure up to 2m (6ft) in diameter. Their purpose is unclear and it is not known how these indigenous people managed to transport spheres weighing several tons to the Isla del Coco, some 20km (12 miles) offshore. The artefacts of the *indigenas* can be seen at many of the museums in San José. There is also an important archaeological site at the Monumento Nacional Guayabo, some 85km (53 miles) to the east of San José. Excavations continue, funded by a small tax on exported bananas.

Below Animal figures, carved by indigenous craftsmen, are on sale in tourist shops in Monteverde. There has been a revival in locally produced handicrafts.

Above A lithic sphere or stone ball, made by the Diquis tribe in southwest Costa Rica. These curious artefacts, made of granite, are sought-after garden ornaments today.

THE SPANISH CONQUEST

The influence of the Spanish can be traced back to 1502, when Christopher Columbus, on his fourth voyage to the New World, landed at what is now Puerto Limón. Columbus noted that the natives were friendly and were generously bedecked with gold jewellery. Mistakenly believing that the country was enormously rich in gold and other precious minerals, Columbus named the land Costa Rica. There were frequent attempts by the Spaniards to colonize the land over the next few decades. Many of these ventures failed due to the harsh landscape and resistance of the *indigenous* people. The conquest, nevertheless, was eventually completed by the 1560s, helped by the spread of common diseases brought by the Europeans, which decimated the *indigenas*, whose numbers dropped to barely 10,000.

Above On his fourth voyage to the New World, Christopher Columbus discovered Costa Rica in 1502. Filled with hope, he named it the Rich Coast, but the natives had bartered their gold with people from other parts of Central America.

The colonists eventually found that the Central Valley (essentially a high plateau) with its healthy climate and fertile soil was the ideal place to settle. This remote area was, however, largely isolated from mainstream Spanish culture, making trade difficult. The settlers, therefore, were obliged to resort to subsistence farming like the indigenas before them. With so few native people, the colonists were unable to use slaves or to inter-marry and set up the mestizo culture that is such a feature in many other parts of Latin America. It is claimed that these factors were responsible for the egalitarian society that exists in Costa Rica today.

INDEPENDENCE

In 1823, along with other Central American countries, Costa Rica gained its independence from Spain. This freedom was not, however, without its threats. In 1855, an American adventurer, William Walker, arrived in the area with a band of mercenaries intent on turning the whole of Central America into a slave colony. Costa Rica raised a ragtag army of 9000 civilians, many armed with little more than farming implements. They defeated Walker and his men just over the Nicaraguan border. The hero of the hour was a young drummer boy named Juan Santamaría, who torched the fort where Walker was holding out, dying in a hail of bullets.

The first democratic elections were held in 1889, with the vote extending from the richest coffee baron to the poorest *campesino*. Women and blacks waited until 1949 for the franchise.

Democracy was underpinned by a stable economy, supported by coffee exports to Europe.

In 1890 a railway line was completed between San José and the Caribbean coast. Known as the Jungle Train, it took 20 years to construct and cost the lives of over 4000 workers. Towards the end of the project, an American engineer, Minor Keith, began to grow bananas to finance the last few miles of the track. The plantations proved remarkably successful and bananas became an important export crop. Keith then formed the United Fruit Company, which was to revolutionize labour relations and have important social and economic implications, both in Costa Rica and in the rest of Central America.

THE 20TH CENTURY

The two world wars had little effect on Costa Rica, apart from hitting coffee exports.

Hostilities, however, came to the country in 1948, when a defeated candidate in the presidential election refused to accept the result. Civil war

Above This is the statue of Juan Santamaría in Alajuela, the drummer boy who died in 1855 resisting the army of the American freebooter William Walker, who had a grand scheme to establish slavery in Central America.

ensued and a junta briefly took over the country. A new constitution was eventually drafted, giving votes to women and blacks and abolishing the armed forces. This was the foundation of the modern Costa Rican state and was to lead to decades of peaceful government. In contrast, many Central American neighbours were engaged in political conflict during the 1970s and 80s. In 1986, the Costa Rican president, Oscar Arias Sánchez, formulated a peace plan to bring stability to the region. He was rewarded with the Nobel Peace prize.

GOVERNMENT AND THE ECONOMY TODAY

Governments are elected by proportional representation every four years, with some 57 deputies each representing 30,000 people. Executive power is in the hands of a president. Neither deputies nor president can serve for more than one four-year term successively. Voting is mandatory and election days are public holidays.

The economy is based on the export of agricultural produce, such as coffee and bananas. Trade is overwhelmingly with the United States, although there are increasing exports to Europe. Since 1990, the main source of foreign income has been tourism, with over one million visitors contributing annually. Costa Rica is now one of the world's most popular countries for eco-tourism. Costa Rica is a model for other developing countries. Its economy is diverse, inflation is under control and debt has been greatly reduced. It disbanded its armed forces in 1949 and the money saved is ploughed back into education, health and the social services.

Opposite A coffee plantation on the rolling hills of the Central Valley. The rich volcanic soils encouraged production and coffee is now the country's leading export, and second only to tourism as a source of income.

16

San José

Costa Rica's capital, San José, lies at a height of around 1100m (3601ft) in the Central Valley, enjoying what many people claim to be one of the world's very best climates. Founded in 1737, it is now home to over 300,000 *Josefinos*. The modern central area of the city has a strong North American flavour, with a grid-type street plan, a filigree of overhead power lines, colourful neon signs, many fast-food outlets and chronic traffic jams. In contrast, some of the suburbs, such as Otoya and Amon, have leafy avenues and fine colonial architecture.

Above A panoramic view of the office blocks and skyscrapers that form the central business district of Costa Rica's capital, San José. Volcanic mountains form a dramatic backdrop.

Left A street trader offers his wares of beads, cheap jewellery and trinkets. His business is supported by the growth in tourism.

Opposite Market stalls laden with fresh, locally grown fruit and vegetables in the Coca Cola district of San José, make an ideal spot to pick up items for a picnic.

Above Avenida Central is the main pedestrianized shopping area in San José, where you often see businessmen chatting during their lunch breaks.

Left The fountain in San José's Central Park is flanked by the Metropolitan Cathedral and the Melico Salazar Theatre. Nearby you will find Avenida Central, which is the main shopping thoroughfare.

Right A young boy looks after his fruit stall. Education is compulsory up to the age of 14, but many children work to help support their families.

Above Dominating the east side of Central Park is the whitewashed and columnar front of the Metropolitan Cathedral. The interior has a barrel arched ceiling, but little of the baroque features that typify most of Costa Rica's churches. The present building replaced the original cathedral felled by an earthquarke in 1821.

Left Gaudy, flashing neon signs advertise everything from cigarettes to beer and hangover cures, helping to give the impression of a typical American city. Night life can be quite vibrant, with busy restaurants, bars, clubs and discos.

Opposite Detail of the interior of the National Theatre shows décor that was done at great expense by the finest craftsmen from Europe using marble, hardwood and gold leaf. Italian painters worked on the ceilings and murals, one of which was depicted on the old five colon note.

Above Located on the 11th floor of an office block, San José's Jade Museum has one of the best collections of jade in the world. Jade is valued for its rarity as there are only six known quarries in the world. There are stunning views of the city from the museum's windows.

Left The increase in tourism in recent years is evident with this tram in San José City's streets. They provide a quick, easy and cheap way to see the main sights of the central area.

Opposite Lithic spheres, military relics and specimens of Costa Rica's common trees and shrubs can be seen in the grounds of the National Museum, which occupies the now redundant Bellavista army barracks.

Following pages San José's National Theatre was built in the 1980s after a visiting opera singer refused to perform, as there was no suitable venue. The coffee barons had raised the revenue for a theatre by putting a tax on their own coffee bags.

The Central Valley

The Central Valley, Costa Rica's most heavily populated area, is the location of four provincial capitals – Alajuela, Cartago, Heredia and San José plus a host of attractive towns and villages. Few tourists miss the craft village of Sarchí. The church at Grecia, made of earthquake-proof steel plates, is also notable. This region is surrounded by high mountain ranges, liberally scattered with active and dormant volcanoes. Some, such as Volcán Poás and Volcán Irazú with its pea-green crater lake, are easily accessible.

Above Bromeliads are the most popular flowers at the Lankester Botanical Gardens. Set up by an English biologist, Charles Lankester, the gardens are now administered by the University of Costa Rica.

Left Local guides and sightseers on a rainforest aerial tram, which travels through the jungle canopy in the Braulio Carrillo National Park near Heredia over a 2.6km (1.6-mile) course. A wide range of birds and butterflies can be seen close up.

Opposite In other areas of Costa Rica the rain forest canopy can be seen from special aerial walkways, which offer intimate close-up views of plants, animals and insects.

Right There are many traditional, gaily painted ox carts in the village of Sarchí. Miniature ox carts are popular souvenirs for tourists. The designs are thought to have originated in Andalucía.

Opposite The Basilica de Nuestra Señora de los Angeles at Cartago, which houses *La Negrita*, Costa Rica's black patron saint. The original cathedral was destroyed in the 1926 earthquake and rebuilt in Byzantine style. There is an annual pilgrimage on 2 August to celebrate *La Negrita*.

Below Pottery is also made in the craft village of Sarchí. The main street is lined with artisans' workshops and tasteful retail outlets selling a range of locally made objects.

Right Outdoor adventure activities are becoming increasingly popular in Costa Rica. Here, a group of white water rafters braves the Huscas rapids along the Pacuaré River.

Opposite Catarata La Paz or Peace Waterfall is some 50km (32 miles) north of San José. The Rio La Paz cascades around 1400m (4593ft) down the flanks of Volcán Poás ending in a dramatic waterfall. The adventurous at heart can follow a short trail that leads behind the plunging water.

Below A popular excursion is to the summit of Volcán Poás, which is a gentle 200m (656ft) walk from the car park. Poás, which last had a minor eruption in 1989, still emits gas and steam, while occasional rumbles can close the area to visitors. The upper slopes are covered with dwarf cloud forest.

Above Ujarras is famous as the site of the ruined church of Nuestra Señora de la Limpia Concepción, which dates from the late 17th century. Noted for some bizarre miracles, the church was abandoned in 1833 after the region was severely flooded.

Opposite Grecia's crimson coloured church is made of steel plates that have been riveted together. The building material is effective against distruction by earthquakes – the fate of an earlier church on the site.

Right A brightly coloured poison-arrow frog in the forest around La Selva Biological Research Station. These tiny frogs, some of which are as small as your little finger, can exude toxins that can cause paralysis and even death in animals as well as humans.

Following pages An attractive waterfall cascades through luxuriant tropical plants in the grounds of the Tabacón Hot Springs Resort near Fortuna. The stream rises on the slopes of Volcán Arenal and provides warm water bathing.

The Pacific Coast

The Pacific coast offers strong contrasts. In the north, where the dry tropical forest has largely been cleared for cattle ranching, *sabaneros* (cowboys) are a familiar sight. Here, a long dry season has encouraged the growth of tourism. The old colonial town of Liberia is the main centre of the north, its new airport attracting increasing amounts of international traffic. Further south along this coast the climate becomes wet and humid, perfect for banana and oil palm plantations. Here lies Costa Rica's most popular nature reserve – the Manuel Antonio National Park. Dense tropical forest near the Panamanian border holds much potential for future ecological tourist development.

Above There is a statue of a mermaid on the beach at Jacó, along the Pacific coast. Jacó is the nearest coastal resort to San José and very popular with *Josefinos* during weekends. The main street is lively with boutiques, bars and surf shops.

Left Appealing little mud crabs are common along the mangrove-lined creeks of the Pacific coast. They are preyed on by racoons and when disturbed they scuttle off back to their holes in the mud.

Opposite Walkers stroll along an empty beach in Manuel Antonio National Park. The beach is backed by a luxuriant rainforest, which is inhabited by a host of birds and mammals such as sloths, armadillos and agoutis. All four species of Costa Rican monkeys can be found here.

Opposite Horse riding is a popular pastime in Costa Rica and visitors can hire horses at many locations. Here, a rider takes horses along the beautiful sandy beach near Manuel Antonio National Park in the south-west of the country. Towering clouds and offshore islands complete the alluring picture.

Right Life is full of hazards for a baby turtle. Despite being protected, many eggs are taken by humans and a variety of animals. As the hatchlings make for the sea they run the gauntlet of hungry gulls, vultures and frigate birds. Once in the open ocean they are food for barracudas and sharks. Only a small fraction reach maturity.

Below On the beaches of Costa Rica, you will find the nesting ground of the giant leatherback, *Dermochelys coriacea*, which is the most spectacular turtle. Often weighing over a ton, its carapace (shell) can measure up to 1.6m (5ft) long, making it the largest reptile in the world. Watching such a giant creature leave the sea and lumber up the beach to lay its eggs is truly a memorable experience.

Opposite Ranchers on horseback drive their cattle over the savanna-like landscape of Guanacaste province. The ranchers, or *sabaneros,* have a distinct cowboy culture that is every bit as evocative as the American Wild West.

Left Squirrel monkeys are the smallest, rarest and most endangered of the Costa Rican monkeys. Delightfully coloured, half their size is taken up by their long prehensile tails. They spend the day in small family groups, jumping from tree to tree in search of food. Squirrel monkeys are confined to small areas of the Manuel Antonio and Corcovado national parks.

Below A camping site at Corcovado on the Osa Peninsula in the south west of Costa Rica. Corcovado, the remotest part of the country, is rich in wildlife and only gradually developing as an eco-tourist destination.

Above A truck on the Pan American Highway that runs through the entire length of Costa Rica. This highway not only links central American countries, but also links the region to North and South America.

Opposite Tourists enjoy boat rides across the Sierpe River in south-west Costa Rica. The river is navigable for 30km (19 miles) upstream. Lodges provide opportunities for fishing, hiking and horseback riding.

Right Iguanas are common in Costa Rica. A female, on average, lays 50 papery-skinned eggs at a time, and may breed twice a year.

Opposite *Ticos* enjoy a game of football on the beach at Playas del Coco. They are obsessed with soccer, which is a major sport in Costa Rica. Leagues operate from September to June, which enables star players to perform in Europe during the winter season.

Left A dolphin bow-rides alongside a boat in Golfo Dulce in the south-west of the country. Whale and dolphin watching are becoming an increasingly popular activity among tourists.

Following pages Manuel Antonio National Park, on the Pacific coast, is the smallest, most visited park in the country and visitor numbers are restricted daily to protect the abundant wildlife.

Below Sail fishing out of Puerto Jiménez in the Golfo Dulce, Península de Osa. Sport fishing is particularly popular with American tourists, as Costa Rican waters teem with tarpon, marlin and wahoo.

The Caribbean Coast

The hot, wet Caribbean coast was once remote and sparsely populated, but since the building of the 'Jungle Railway' in the late 19th century, the completion of the Guápiles Highway in the 1980s and the increasing use of air routes, the region has been opened up and tourism is gradually taking hold. The first area to develop was the Tortuguero National Park. Further north, the Barra del Colorado Wildlife Refuge, mainly used for sport fishing at present, has even more potential. The main town and port of the Caribbean coast is Puerto Limón, famous for its vibrant annual Carnival.

Above The filigree pattern of a spiders' web is commonly seen around the Tortuguero National Park. Over 35,000 species of insects have been recorded in Costa Rica.

Left A three-toed sloth, *Bradypus tridactylus*, hangs from a basket. Sloths have a low metabolism and are so slow moving that moss and lichen grow on their coats. The best place to spot sloths is in the Cecropia trees that grow along the river banks.

Opposite Palm trees grow beside the Rio Reventazón near Jungle Lodge, in the Tortuguero National Park. A number of lodges in the Tortuguero area provide exciting rainforest experiences for visitors.

Opposite Giant buttresses at the base of a Ceiba tree in the Caño Negro Wildlife Refuge near the border with Nicaragua. The reserve covers around 10,000ha (24,700 acres). It is rarely visited, but teems with birds, reptiles and animals.

Left Leaf cutter ants are often seen marching along the forest floor carrying pieces of leaf to their underground colony. The leaves are left to decay into mulch on which fungus grows to feed the colony, which may number over a million.

Below A percussion band beats out its rhythm during the annual carnival in Limón on Columbus Day, the second Monday of October. It lasts for a week and brings over 100,000 people to the area. The attractions include street bands, craft stalls, folk dancing, beauty contests, bull running, and fireworks.

Right A small boat at a building yard on the Tortuguero river, which is part of the Intra Coastal Waterway that runs parallel to the Caribbean and is a major line of communication through the Tortuguero rainforest.

Left Green iguanas, which can grow up to 2m (7ft) in length, are usually spotted on the riverbanks of the Costa Rican forests. Now an endangered species, they are often sold as exotic pets.

Below A fishing canoe beaches and the fishermen land their catch of the day. Fish does not feature strongly in Costa Rican cuisine, since much of the catch is exported, but you can generally find *ceviche* (raw fish in lime juice), *pargo* (red snapper) and *corvine* (sea bass) on the menu.

Below The palm-fringed beach at Puerto Viejo has become very popular with surfing and backpacking crowds. The main attraction is the Salsa Brava wave which crashes ashore at its best between December and March, and is definitely for the experts.

Above Tourists can enjoy a good cooked meal from the local food vendors in Puerto Limón. Creole cooking, which features strongly along the Caribbean coast, is much spicier than the usual Costa Rican food.

Following pages Puerto Limón becomes deserted as the sky darkens. The container trade has moved to nearby Moín and it now deals mainly with cruise liners.

Below A young boy takes a refreshing drink of coconut milk. Coconuts are often on sale at the roadside. Both the milk of the coconut and its flesh are essential ingredients in Creole cooking.

The National Parks

Costa Rica's national parks system was established in the 1960s and today there are over 20 of them, some of which also protect physical features such as cave systems, beaches and volcanoes. Add the wildlife refuges, biological reserves and privately owned sanctuaries and you find that an impressive 25% of the country's area is protected in some way. Most of the larger parks are surrounded by buffer zones where a certain amount of activity, such as logging, is permitted, but in future it is planned to join some of the parks to create large 'corridors' for the movement of wildlife.

Above The damp atmosphere of the Monteverde Cloud Forest Reserve encourages vegetation, with epiphytes, lianas and mosses in profusion among the 2500 plant species identified here. This is the best place to see Costa Rica's exotic bird, the resplendent quetzal.

Right The keel-billed toucan, *Ramphastos sulfuratus*, is one of six types of toucan found in Costa Rica. Identified by their large bills, these birds have an unmusical call and live in the forest canopy where they feed on fruit, seeds, insects, lizards and small snakes.

Opposite A river cascades over rocks in the steamy atmosphere of the Corcovado National Park. It is the most remote of the country's parks, consisting largely of rainforest.

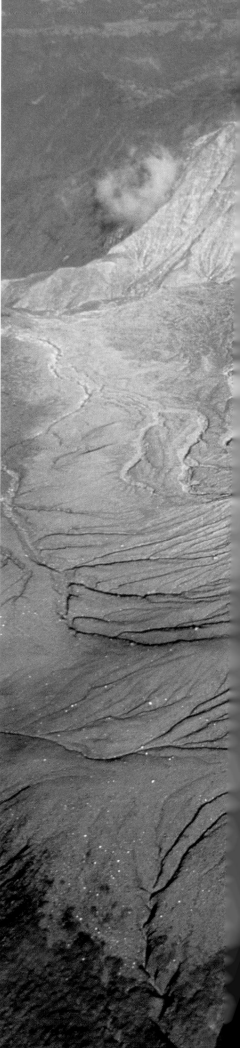

Above Volcán Arenal is everyone's idea of what a volcano should look like. Rising to 1633m (5358ft), it has a perfect cone shape and plumes of smoke. Volcanic ash has produced a rich soil that encourages luxuriant vegetation in the surrounding national park.

Right An aerial view of the main crater of Volcán Poás showing recent lava flows and gullies etched into the volcanic ash. It erupted in 1989 and its crater is claimed to be one of the largest in the world.

Below The Rincón de la Vieja National Park in Guanacaste province displays a variety of volcanic features, such as the gurgling mud pool shown here. Also to be seen are minor craters, hot springs, small geysers and fumeroles.

Opposite Palm trees make an exotic backdrop on Cahuita beach at sunrise. The small national park here covers a mere 1067ha (2636 acres) and consists of rainforest, mangrove swamps and an offshore coral reef. Many different animals are found in this tiny area.

Right Black Howler monkeys, *Alouatta pigra*, are found in most of the forested national parks. Said to have the loudest voices in the animal world, they will roar loudly at intruders on their territory.

Left An armadillo, *Dasypus novemcinctus*, forages on the forest floor in Cahuita National Park. Armadillos are nocturnal, have poor eyesight and have been known to blunder into stationary observers.

Below A diver explores the colourful coral reef in the Cahuita National Park.

Above A beach camp filled with hammocks in the Corcovado National Park on the Osa Peninsula. Nesting grounds for four turtle species can be seen on the beaches of Corcovado, while sharks and barracudas patrol offshore.

Left Tourists hike on one of the many trails through the rainforest of Corcovado National Park. The dense vegetation shelters many endangered species such as the scarlet macaw, harpy eagle, squirrel monkey and jaguar.

Below The hot and wet atmosphere provides ideal conditions for the growth of fungi. There are thousands of exotic and colourful species to be seen throughout the forest.

Left Bird watching from the tree canopy in the Corcovado National Park is a naturalist's delight. The park covers 42,000ha (104,000 acres) of primary forest and there is plenty for visitors to see: 500 species of trees, 400 different birds, 139 types of mammals and over 100 species of amphibians and reptiles.

Above The Skywalk at Monteverde Cloud Forest Reserve has 1000m (3280ft) of paths. It includes five suspended bridges that have been built through various levels of the forest, giving an unparalleled close encounter with nature.

Left A long-tailed hermit hummingbird, *Phaethornis superciliosus*, hovers to collect nectar from a flower. Over 50 species of hummingbirds have been recorded in Costa Rica. They hover by beating their wings over 80 times a second, which even enables them to fly backwards.

Right The growth of fungus on a fallen log helps the decaying process of the biomass in La Amistad National Park. La Amistad is an international peace park and a UNESCO World Heritage site. It extends on both sides of the border with Panama.

Opposite Tourists usually stop for a meal and a drink while travelling on the long road to Volcán Poás National Park. The walls and counter of this pub are festooned with currency notes and visiting cards from all over the world.

Opposite Giant leaves can be found in the cloud forest· close to Volcán Irazú. The constant humidity encourages growth. The cloud forests, with their mist-shrouded ridges, valleys and streams, have a feel of mystery.

Below Visitors can view the main crater of Volcán Irazú with its pea-green lake. Good visibility is essential for viewing this volcano, and sometimes in the early morning it is possible to see both the Pacific and Caribbean coasts from the summit.

Following pages Mangrove forests are found on both of Costa Rica's shorelines. There are many types of mangrove tree, but all are typified by aerial roots.

Coffee Growing

The first coffee beans were brought to Costa Rica from Jamaica in 1779 and within a few years coffee growing became firmly established. Until the 1990s, when it was overtaken by tourism, it was Costa Rica's main export earner. Conditions in the Central Valley are ideal and the beans grown here are among the best in the world. Coffee production has brought great wealth to the larger producers, whose labourers are often poorly paid. In addition there are many small-scale farmers who can suffer badly from the fluctuations in world prices.

Above Coffee berries are harvested from November to January. The picking season begins with a festival and picking tournament.

Right Coffee berries grow close to the main stem of the plant, which makes for easy picking. The plants are from pure Arabica stock, which were brought by the Spanish to Costa Rica via North Africa, Cuba and Jamaica.

Opposite Coffee plantations on the rolling landscape of the Central Valley's well-drained slopes benefit from the rich, well-drained volcanic soil. Shade trees are now being reintroduced, helping America's songbirds, which spend the winter here. You can now buy 'songbird-friendly coffee'.

Opposite Local men collect coffee berries from bushes in the farming community of Finca Anael. Each berry contains two coffee beans.

Right The coffee beans are a grey-green colour when are they laid out to dry in the sun. They are frequently raked over at this stage.

Below As part of the Café Britt tour, visitors are taken around the plantation to see the coffee shrubs and to experience the growing conditions for themselves. The guides are all multilingual estate workers.

Following pages Smaller coffee producers suffer enormously from fluctuations in the price of coffee, so they usually diversify by growing a variety of other crops and keeping a few farm animals.

Copyright rests with the following photographers and/or their agents. Key to Locations: t = top; tl = top left; tr = top right; b = bottom; bl = botto
left; br = bottom right; l = left; r = right; c = centre; cl = centre left; cr = centre right. (No abbreviation is given for pages with a single image, or page
on which all photographs are by same photographer.)

AA	AA World Travel Library	**JD**	James Davis	**PP**	Papilio Photos
BC	Brett Cole	**JS**	Jeroen Snijders Fotografie	**SC**	Sue Cunningham/SCP
DD	Diana Dicker	**KS**	Kevin Schafer	**SCPL**	Sylvia Cordaiy Photo Library
DGP	www.deepgreenphotography.com	**KY**	Keith Young/Cape Photo Library	**TI**	www.travel-ink.co.uk
FF	Ffotograff/Fabienne Fossez	**LAY**	Lou Anne Young/iAfrica Photos		(AH= Angela Hampton; CB=Chris Barton;
FK	Fred Kamphues	**LW**	Lawson Wood		DF=David Forman; GB=Grazyna Bonati;
FM	France Maher/iAfrica Photos	**ME**	Mary Evans Photo Library		RR=Roger Rowland)
HA	Harryhaussen/Alamy	**MM**	Matt May Photography	**VE**	Victor Engelbert
HPL	Hutchison Photo Library	**PA**	Photo Access		

1		AA	13	b	JS	30	b	JS	47		AA	65	tr	PP
2	t	MM	14	t	SC	31		JS	48-49		FK	65	b	LW
2	b	DGP	14	b	SC	32		VE	50	t	KS	66		A
3		FM	15		ME	33	t	KS	50	b	FM	67	t	FF
4	t	KS	16	t	VE	33	b	TIDF	51		TIDF	67	b	KY
4	b	SC	17		JD	34	t	TIGB	52	t	JS	68	t	FF
5	t	HA	18	t	JS	34	b	KS	52	b	FM	68	b	KS
5	b	BC	18	b	LAY	35		SC	53		KS	69	t	JS
6	t	PP	19		AA	36-37		MM	54	t	KS	69	b	KS
6	b	PP	20		PA	38	t	MM	54	b	DD	70		LAY
7	t	SCPL	21	t	SC	38	b	TIAH	55		LAY	71	t	JS
7	b	KS	21	b	AA	39		KS	56		JS	71	b	TIRR
8	t	DGP	22	t	SC	40		AA	57	t	FM	72-73		JS
8	b	DGP	22	b	AA	41	t	KS	57	b	DGP	74	t	DGP
9	t	DGP	23		JS	41	b	KS	58-59		FM	74	b	SC
9	b	FM	24	t	JS	42	t	PP	60	t	KS	75		AA
10	t	SC	24	b	LAY	42	b	FF	60	b	BC	76		AA
10	b	FM	25		DD	43		AA	61		AA	77	t	HPL
11	t	FM	26-27		PA	44		JS	62	t	KS	77	b	JS
11	b	AA	28	t	DGP	45	t	AA	62	b	TICB	78-79		LAY
12	t	JS	28	b	AA	45	b	SCPL	63		KS			
12	b	SC	29		KS	46	t	KS	64		KS			
13	t	FM	30	t	TIGB	46	b	KS	65	tl	PP			

First published in 2004 by
New Holland Publishers Ltd
London • Cape Town
Sydney • Auckland
www.newhollandpublishers.com

86 Edgware Road, London, W2 2EA
United Kingdom

80 McKenzie Street, Cape Town, 8001
South Africa

14 Aquatic Drive, Frenchs Forest, NSW 2086
Australia

218 Lake Road, Northcote, Auckland
New Zealand

ISBN 1 84330 999 8 (hb)
1 84537 000 7 (pb)

Publisher Mariëlle Renssen
Publishing managers Claudia Dos Santos,
Simon Pooley
Commisioning Editor: Alfred LeMaitre
Cartographer Carl Germishuys
Designer Elmari Kuyler
Editor Nicky Steenkamp
Picture researcher Karla Kik
Production Myrna Collins
Proofreader Anna Tanneberger

Reproduction by Unifoto (Pty) Ltd
Printed and bound in Singapore by
Tien Wah Press (Pte) Ltd

10 9 8 7 6 5 4 3 2 1

JADINE